WONDERLAND IN ALICE
PLUS OTHER WAYS OF SEEING

Poetry By Paul Brookes

With A Foreword By Ian McMillan
Illustrated By Jane Cornwell

Jane's
Studio Press

WONDERLAND IN ALICE
PLUS OTHER WAYS OF SEEING

Written by Paul Brookes
With a foreword by Ian McMillan
Illustrated by Jane Cornwell
Edited by Susan Richardson

Jane's Studio Press
Design & illustration by Jane Cornwell
www.janecornwell.co.uk

ISBN: 978-1-7398281-0-3
E-book available.

Jane's
Studio Press

ACKNOWLEDGMENTS

"In The Nod" first published in Medium's *Literally Literary*.

Thankyou to Sarah Connor for publishing "Our Spired Unicorn" on her poetry advent calendar in 2020. It first appeared with its counterpart "Our Unicorn Spired" in my Ekphrastic Challenge 2020. and later on in steadfast Glynn Young's *Faith, Fiction, Friends Saturday.* Thank you to the stunning artist that contributed to it: Jane Cornwell.

"The Says" originally appeared in *Glomag*, July 2017. Thankyou, Glory.

Thankyou for Ian McMillan's solid support of my writing from my first pamphlet onwards and for the honour of his foreward to this book.

Poems For All accepted "In The Nod Of This" for publication. It's PFA #1573 in 2017.

"A Wonder" appeared in the late *Open Mouse* in 2016.

"Stylite" first appeared in *Visual Verse*.

I was honoured beyond measure when Jane Cornwell invited me to publish with her small press. Her art is always memorable and inspirational. Thank you very much to my editor Susan Richardson for her excellent skills, guidance and constructive comments.

This book is dedicated to my late Mam. On my first experience of writer's block when I was young and school homework was for a nonsense poem about an animal she wrote one for me called, if I recall correctly: "The Elephant With A Propeller For A Nose."

Paul Brookes

This book is dedicated to my daughter, Beth, who kindly allowed me to draw her as 'Alice.' Like Paul, Beth finds magic and mystery in everything.

Jane Cornwell

CONTENTS

Wonderland In Alice

Through Alice And What The Looking Glass Found There

FOREWORD
INSIDE THE WORLD OF PAUL BROOKES

One of the jobs a poet has to do, it seems to me, is to create a world and encourage us all to live in it. The world will be like that thing that people call 'The Real World' but it will be shinier, more thoughtful, more open to interpretation, more multi-dimensional.

As a poet Paul Brookes is a superb world builder; in his work the ordinary becomes extraordinary and, if we take our time with it, his world can become our world too.

Listen to this world speaking. Inanimate objects and abstractions speak here; rocks and skies and gusts of wind have vocabularies and syntaxes that challenge us to think. South Yorkshire speaks here, in its own dialect but also in its history-ravaged post-industrialism. Here are new folk tales, freshly minted but seemingly ancient and modern at the same time, speaking to our world through the prism of theirs.

There's a sequence at the heart of the book which is a series of variations on and explorations of the world of Alice in Wonderland which plays with language and ideas and presents us with vivid ways of re-entering a world we think we know well, and the sequence as a whole is prime example of Paul Brookes' poetic skill of leading us down rabbit holes to linguistic tea parties we will never want to leave.

Enjoy this collection!

Ian McMillan

STYLITE

With a clear sky I can see for miles.
I try to catch the bread and wine

thrown upwards as if the lobbers
feel once caught all their prayers are answered.

What is it about folk who decide to be alone
in caves, on mountains on tall pillars,

cut themselves off from the nine to five,
regular grind blistered in sun,

buffeted by gusts, pelted hailstone,
rain sodden, bloodied by ice,

and oiled young bucks in gangs who wang
stones to dislodge me from this precipice,

seethe at my chosen difference,
see a hoity fella puts himself

above others, show off, poseur,
while others try to tempt me

as if I'm in a desert, promise money,
fleshly pleasures if only I come down

off my pedestal? Close my eyes, hear
city hawkers and hustlers, icecream

vans musical wind up and down streets,
prayer call of mosques, toll of iron bells.

when gust alters direction inhale,
fish from the docks, sewerage farm stink,

grit blown from dusty roads in my teeth,
seasalt laps this dry tongue, breathe in

garlic evenings, curried afternoons,
fragrant citrus trees, feminine perfume,

spring blossom amid morning birdsong
at a change of season. All are prayers.

OUR UNICORN SPIRE

rises from the head
of a wild, untameable animal
with frozen strength and agility.

As a schoolboy I placed
paper over a stone in the walls
built to hold this force,

asked to rub with coloured pencils,
or chalk to get the complex
lines and changes I was more

distracted open mouthed at the horn spire.
We entered the beast at Easter,
Harvest and Christmas.

Sometimes its insides were full
of flowers and fruits, or holly
and candles. Mam said *Unicorns*

don't exist, and showed me pictures
of Narwhal and Rhinoceros. The village
church was more magical than those.

My unicorn was frozen
into stone and villagers hollowed
it out to make a church.

I still remember the teacher
asking me why I hadn't finished
my stone rubbing. I stayed stum,

afraid of being called 'silly;'
or 'he's in his own world, again.'
It was wonderful having my school

next to a petrified creature.
When we studied fossils,
I wanted to point to the church.

I wanted to rub my hands over its flanks,
Imagined it breathing, knew graveyard walls
could not imprison it forever.

The Gust Says

Enough. I'm sick
of being the only one

who moves things about.
It's regime change.

I will not be moved. Dust,
leaves, cans, paper will

have to move themselves.
Windfarms using my service

without a thought to what
I want. Waves too. Totally

oblivious to my needs.
It's an effort to stay still,

but I will do it. I'm no longer
the wind of change. Do it

yourselves. How do you
make a difference?

Put your lips together
and blow.

The Rocks Say

Enough! Years we've let you

walk all over, clamber
all over, stab us with
steel pinions to secure
your sense of comfort.

It's time for us to forego
this malaise and move
like stone giants
in your legends.

Stretch our legs, work
these tired sinews.
We're doing you a favour.

We warn you. So you can
become refugees
Once your home
is rubble and you flee
the fires and explosions,

As if we've declared war
on you, when all I
do is move.

The Skies Say

Enough! You go through us.
You really do.

We're all air to you. All clouds
and flitting. Our colours
and appearance pushed about
by Gust, Sun and Moon.

You think we can't stand up
for ourselves. You think
we have no strength of our own.

Be careful!

One time we'll be so still,
even the stars won't move.

One time we'll be so stood
even the sun won't budge.

That day is on its way
over the horizon.

Gust Says Too

I can make hills jump,
and seas hills, I can make you suffer.

You're a bully says the quiet earth.
Gust says *I belong,* then disappears.

Soil shouts *Who to?*
I belong here, to Gust already gone.

Gust returns lifts soil to another place.
Gust tumbled through the grass blades.

I'll spoil your hairdo.
Spread my seeds, replied grass.

I can always redo my hair later.
Gust to rock, *I will wear you down. I swear.*

and promptly forgot what it said.
Gust returned with grit in its teeth
unaware of what it had said.

Gust blew dead leaves into a blazing swirl.
I can make you live again it said.

No reply,
but a rustle from leaves on the tree above.

OUR SPIRED UNICORN

is a place of worship.
A moveable feast beast.

Offer it fruits and flowers
at Harvest, Easter and Christmas.

Baptise bairns, get married,
celebrate the dead in its presence.

Pray before its hooves and flanks,
comb its hair, feed it oats.

Don't try to ride it, or steal its horn.
It is sacred and full of light.

Go where it goes, a disciple.
Some may say you believe in a myth.

Your faith keeps it alive. You
know it as a companion, a friend.

Though it has a life of its own.
Is nothing but itself.

Behind our eyes we are all
mythical beasts to others.

I CAN'T MAKE NEITHER

a head nor tail out of this beast
Who shrugs and our ship yaws.

It's pelt moves up and down beaches
as it shuffles along continents.

I can only see as its curled its face
and tail in sleep and we pitch

over its dreaming, every twitch
a ripple or wave as it hunts,

as we fish its judder, catch scaled insects
that live beneath its slumber.

Clouds get plump on it's visions,
then wander inland to downpour images.

My mates have drowned in its speculations,
overcome by its meanders and cogitations.

They died in its sleep. I shake
at the thought of it awake.

WHEN BEAST COMES OVER THEE

Trogging dahn r streeart
met a wolf going opposite
way

he clambered inside
r marth like it were his
home as he'd abandoned

not long since and climbing
in pissed off ma eagle
and dragon that'd

clawed way over
ma tussiepegs not half
hour since. Reight crowd.

a cud barely speeak.
eagle beddin' dahn
in ma noas

dragon peggin'
in ma balls while
wolf stays in ma gob

BEAUTY AWAKE

Vicious thorns draw her blood,
leave scars , keep her awake.

She wants sleep,
a little sleep. Thorns

grow thick and sharp around her,
block sunlight, so she can barely

see the harsh blades when she moves
to stop her body's cramp.

Suddenly, there is daylight.
A hole in the hedge, and then more.

She hears wood cracking and splitting.
And there he is her saviour.

He cuts away the final branches.
She is free, smiles and nods off.

IN THE NOD OF THIS (Apologies to Oscar Wilde).

land is a giant called Sleep,
and a selfish tree in a selfish garden

that blooms for itself and no one else.
Sleep dreams of a wondrous garden

bedecked with colours rarely seen
in its rainbows and crystals.

In its searches it finds a high wall,
taller than itself. *Perhaps a garden
is behind it,* Sleep muses.

The selfish tree in the selfish garden
hears the rumble of Sleep behind its walls.

The tree encourages the sharp hedge
to grow taller and broader than the wall.

IN THE NOD OF THAT (Apologies to Oscar Wilde).

land is a giant called Sleep,
and a selfish tree in a selfish garden.

The giant Sleep scales the garden walls,
and cries in pain when a thorn

from the taller hedge behind the wall
pricks its finger and blood drops

on flowered earth and blossoms shrivel
as if winter has come to summer.

Sleep sighs, a stream dribbles from its eyes
onto the thorns and the hedge diminishes.

IN THE NOD OF THE OTHER (Apologies to Oscar Wilde).

land is a giant called Sleep,
and a selfish tree in a selfish garden.

A small boy in the garden
sweeps a net to catch butterflies.

He sees the great puddles
of the giant's tears,

the wilted flowers and frozen ground
and so afraid his hand quivers to give

a handkerchief to the sad giant.
The cloth becomes an icicle

in the giant's hands whose smile
becomes a frown at this. In a moment

the boy hugs Sleep whose mouth drops.
The boy is warm and doesn't freeze.

A WONDER (for Barry Hines).

In spring morning haze,
out of a red brick council house,
a bothered standing hawk
steals the wide eyed wonder
of a radged bairn who reaches upwards
with pudgy hands to grasp
her silver underside and blue head.

The wonder bawls as it arcs in her claws
over buried mines and call
centre natter to a high perch
in weed racked ruins of an Old Hall.

The wonder refuses warm remains
of voles and mice,
desperate feathered mam returns
with scavenged chips, naan bread and pizza,

In noon summer shimmer
she pushes wonder to fly,
but it falls out the cup,
grasps stone wall in its drop.

Soon, a cuckoo, wonder heaves
the other nippers out their home,
into an autumn mid afternoon
of burnished fallen leaves,

or, bored at mothers twitter
wonder cannot garner,
breaks its fellow fledglings bones.

Soon too big for home,
wonder falls to earth,
and snaps its spine.

Kestrel mam covers wonder's face
with her wing in winter night
gust, then abandons it
to foxfood and worms.

GODFATHER LIFE

I were born dead.
My father weeps
as he has nowt
and hopes for best.

He holds us out
in middle of our road
and says as whoever
says they want me

can be my godfather.
God turns up first
and says as he can give me
eternal life in heaven.

Dad tells him to bugger off
as I'd still be dead
and he'd still be bereft.
Devil arrives next,

and says he can give me
all riches and principalities
in world at cost of my father's
blood and soul.

Dad tells him to bugger off
as riches were in other things
and he don't want me
withart a father.

Then Life turns up
and says he will make me
a miracle worker and bring
other folk to life. Dad agrees

When I'm of age
Life says to me
I've given you breath
of life you can gi to others.

When you see me not there
it means as they shunt
have it. Don't make me smile.
You won't like it.

If I laugh it will be at you
not with you. You'll have

disobeyed me, so I must
take away your gift.

Then my wife drowns suddenly.
I think surely Life
won't mind, but
it isn't here. I kiss

her lips till they redden.
and there is Life
at the foot of the bed,
and it is smiling.

It says *Well done.*
Pleased to see such progress.
You have challenged me.
I like your spirit. Let

it go this once. Your wife
needs a hug. Then my dad
dies of asphyxiation
in a car accident.

As I am about to give
Dad my breath
Life pulls me away
with an *I know you*

want the best for him.
I reply *If you take*
my gift give it to him.
Life takes my breath away.

1. A RABBIT

A rabbit hole falls into her.
The pocket watch looks at the rabbit
and know it's late.

The big hand claps the little hand
to see such fun.

How will the door enter Alice?
Alice says *I am cake. Eat me.*

The door takes a bite of her hand.
It grows and grows

I am too big to enter you, now,
says the door.

I am a bottle. Drink me,
answers Alice.

The door sups her
and enters her.

2. SHUFFLE

A pack of playing cards
decide to play inside her.

They shuffle her into black
and red, divide her into suits,

Her heart becomes diamonds
Her hands spades,
Her legs clubs
Her torso hearts.

Alice says *Off with her head!*
to the Queen of her heart,
but the Queen topples
the suits and escapes.

Alice has two thumbs:
Tweedledee and Tweedledum
she twiddles in thought.

3. TEA PARTY

Teapot is fast asleep
curled inside the dormouse
curled inside Alice

Her table lays the cloth.
The cloth places the teapot,
cups and saucers.
A hat and watch sit on
the only two chairs.

Take a seat.
They say in chorus.

There are no seats
Alice answers.

All the seats taken then.

Is it the month of your time?
Ask the hat and the watch.

It's ALWAYS the month of my time
while I'm alive.

You ought to eat and drink less.
You'll get fat.

I have had my fill, she replies.
You haven't had anything.

Less is more, she answers
and leaves the table
inside her.

4. THE DOOR

Suddenly she feels the alarm
of the biological pocket watch
inside her.

Where, o where could they be.
O, my little hand, o my big hand.
Alice will kill me if I can't find her
bracelet and mobile.

Alice wants to say she has those
already but searches her pockets
and can't find anything.

A door sits beside her
as she begins to cry.
Through her tears she sees
a painting of a tree on the door.

Soon her tears make waves,
she swims, but her arms
get tired, so she clambers
on the door where she is dry.

She thinks she fell asleep
and opens the tree on the door
and finds herself on the naughty step
of some stairs and a voice says:

Is that you, Alice? You spend
far too much time outside.
Go inside and get some fresh
air and vitamin D from the sun.

She checks her wrist and pockets
and sighs. The tears
must have washed the bracelet
back on her wrist, mobile in her pocket.

5. THE MUSHROOM

sits on a caterpillar
behind Alice's eyes

The mushroom engrossed
in its mobile phone,

Alice says to it:
How are you?

I love change too much.
Change isn't quick enough,
Says the mushroom.
This Caterpillar should have
pupated and flown.

Why? Asks Alice.

I'm not sure. You
and I should be wrinklies.
You a middle aged woman,
and I mulch for something
creative and growing.

Time is too slack. Should
buck its ideas up. If you see
it about give what it for from me.

And Alice tries but can get
no more from mobiled mushroom.

6. THE WATCH

She hears the biological pocket watch inside her
say *I'm slow, so slow. I'll be early*
and Alice wants me
not too early, not too late
but prompt. O, my little hand,
my big hand.

In its more haste less speed
Alice sees something drop
from its pocket.

It is a silver nomination bracelet,
and a mobile phone.

Alice picks them up
and shouts after the watch
but it has gone.

So she tries on the bracelet
and it fits. The mobile won't
work because you have
to key in
the correct code.

That'll teach it to look after things,
she thinks.

7. REDUCES.

A court rises in her.
A scroll unfurls and reads from
her biological pocket watch
Tarts have stolen the Knave.

Alice is the judge.
Alice is the Knave.
The judge is the accused.
The accused is the judge.

Testimony transcribes the witnesses.
The spaces between their words testify.

Hat says the party is always ending.
He does not know when
it began to end.

*Off with the head
of the guilty,* Alice says.
Evidence is an atom.

Alice is guilty, says
the heart of the Queen.

Alice feels herself getting smaller.
She cannot see over
her desk.

Alice has disappeared,
says her pocket watch
Everything gets smaller.
Bracelet and mobile left on the chair.

Alice feels these are the worst
days of her death that glorious
Summer afternoon she finds herself
beneath a tree in a stranger place.

1. LOOKING

inside Alice
the looking glass steps
through her.

It sees through her.
The reflection of the mirror
in Alice.

The White Queen
and White King

lift Alice up,

Though to her
they are invisible hands
that make her inside float.

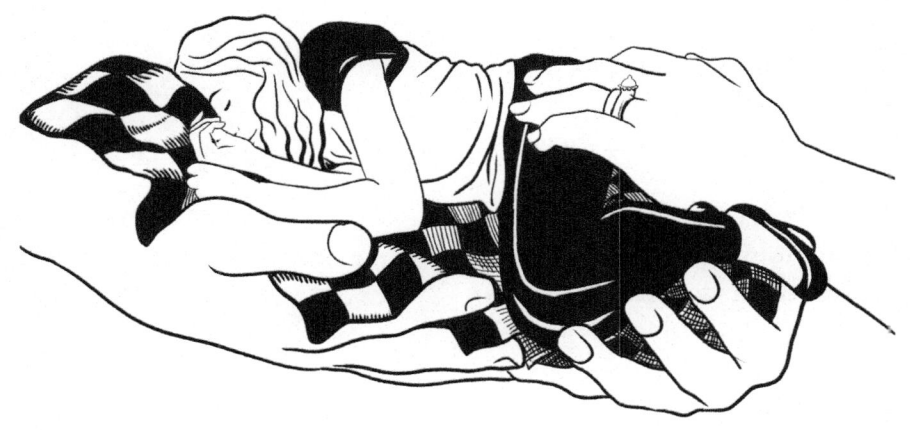

2. FLOWERS

in the garden
shake at the sight of themselves
in Alice's looking glass.

Pink drain to white.
Pale flowers colour up.

The garden path tells
her to stay still
and she'll have adventures.

She lets her feet lead her
up or down the garden path
but arrives where she started.

Alice can't stay still.
She has to move but in moving
always returns to what
she already knows.

I want to have adventures
But nobody'll let me. She complains.

Looks directly at a Rose
And advises it: *Your petals*
are a disgrace. They need
to lean in one direction,
not all directions.

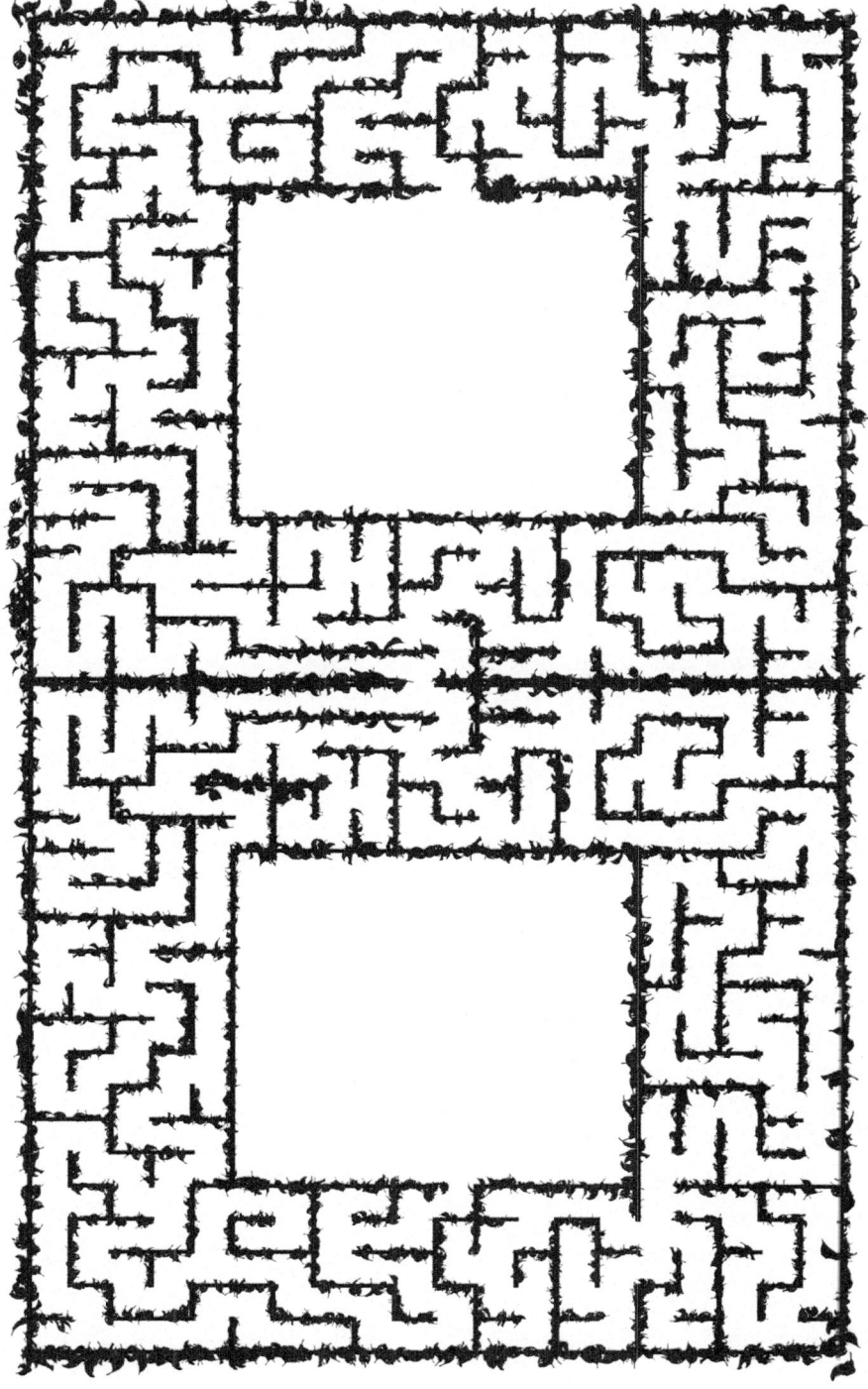

3. ARRIVAL

Alice sees the Red Queen
coming towards her,

but as Alice walks towards her,
she stays the same distance away.

As I say, said the garden path,
If you stay still she'll come to you.

Frustrated, Alice stops where
she is. Suddenly, Red Queen
is by her side and says to her:

There should be more wilderness.
This is far too tidy, organised, my girl.

Look, from this plain mountains
can be valleys.

That's silly, replies Alice.
Psychogeography, says the Queen.

Why did you come into the garden?
You should have stayed outside
In the house.

Exploration, answers Alice,
is best done from an armchair,
where you can get exercise
and fresh air.

4. A SURVEY

To survey the whole scene
You must close your eyes,'
commands the Red Queen

of Alice. *But, then I won't*
be able to see anything.'

You'll be able to see
the whole plan laid out,
replies the Queen.

Alice closes her eyes
hears gust through grass
that is blood through veins,

shiver of trees that is breath
through her lungs,

crumble of soil that is her bones
lengthening,

Scans sheep scattered fields
defined by dry stone walls,
little stone villages beside
rivers tumble into valleys.

Stop dreaming, commands
the Queen. Alice rescans and

sees housing and industrial
estates, warehouses and half

built homes on the fields,
rivers redirected. Soon

these images jog and dash
past, rivers sputter, gust falters,
soil blows away. *I am old*

Alice thinks. Opens her eyes
to find the Red Queen disappeared.

A ticket collector requests her ticket.
I don't have one, she says,

seeing fields pass by a window
of the half empty carriage
A kiss is a ticket says the collector.
Peck, for single, Snog for return.

5. DIGITAL

Highly inappropriate language
In front of a child, Sir.
says a massive voice
beside her ear.

She is a child? asks
the ticket collector
as he plucks out each
of his eyeballs for a scrub.

Forgive me child. My eyes
need a polish.

What's your name?
asks the big voice in her ear.
As she turns her head
Alice smells lilac

and sees a tree above her,
and a small insect on her shoulder.
Alice, she replies to it...
Nice name, answers the insect.

I'm Digital Marketer. You *can*
Call me Digital, says the insect.
Alice was twiddling her thumbs
Tweedledum and Tweedledee.

Ask your opposable thumbs, says Digital.
How..? *Body language. Don't*
ask your other digits, else
You'll be all fingers and thumbs.

6. SIDEWAY

So she holds her thumbs up
to Digital who blends so well
into the background
the insect disappears inside her.

Where am I bound?
She asks her thumbs: Tweedledum
and Tweedledee. They say
together *sideways*

Where is Sideways?
How do I get there?
Diagonally says
Tweedledee,
Slantwise, says
Tweedledum.

Suddenly, a pashmina
blows to her. She wraps it
round her and feels regal.

You're living sideways.
say her thumbs as pashmina
becomes a sheep fleece.
You can trace yourself

back to your source. Your
sauce is Henderson's Relish.
Someone will shake you out
of a bottle in drops.

7. GOOD EGG

Inside her
the sheep fleece falls off
in clumps to show
a fat belly and no neck.

I'm an egg on legs,
she exclaims, then gasps
as she sits on a very high wall
with her little legs dangling.

An odd thought pops
into her head *What or who*
do I make real? I can't make
up myself, can I? All

that we see or seem
is but the real
within the real.

She falls and breaks
into continental plates
ebb and flow
on the shore where

looking glass earth breaks in waves
on the sea, sunset
is dawn and sunrise
night's beginning.

ABOUT PAUL BROOKES

Paul Brookes is a shop assistant. Lives in a cat house full of teddy bears. First play performed at The Gulbenkian Theatre, Hull. His chapbooks include *The Fabulous Invention Of Barnsley*, (Dearne Community Arts, 1993). *A World Where and She Needs That Edge* (Nixes Mate Press, 2017, 2018) *The Spermbot Blues* (OpPRESS, 2017), *Please Take Change* (Cyberwit.net, 2018), *As Folk Over Yonder* (Afterworld Books, 2019). He is a contributing writer of *Literati Magazine* and Editor of *The Wombwell Rainbow Interviews,* book reviews and challenges. Had work broadcast on BBC Radio 3 *The Verb* and videos of his Self Isolation sonnet sequence featured by Barnsley Museums and Hear My Voice Barnsley. He also does photography commissions.

ABOUT THE ILLUSTRATIONS

Paul Brookes and I 'met' when he made an appeal for prompt artwork for a Wombwell Rainbow NAPOWRIMO Ekphrastic Challenge. For me, this was an intriguing new way of working creatively, a mutually inspiring collaborative process with lots of poets and artists worldwide.

This dark fantasy nonsense poetry collaboration with Paul was inspiring and challenging to illustrate. As a child, I hated *Alice in Wonderland*. The 1951 Disney movie scared me so I had no interest in reading anything by Lewis Carroll. When I read Paul's poetry I was intrigued to learn more about Alice. What was the inspiration for Paul's bizarre, disturbing poetry and Lewis Carroll's novels? In 1873 Skeffington Lutwidge, an inspector of asylums in England was killed by an asylum patient. He was the uncle and close friend of Charles Lutwidge Dodgson, also known as Lewis Carroll. In *Alice's Adventures in Wonderland* (1865) and *Through the Looking-Glass, and What Alice Found There* (1871) perhaps trying to make sense of his friend's murder, Lewis Carroll was writing about various forms of mental illness affecting the characters including anxiety, body dysmorphia, narcissism, schizophrenia, obsessive-compulsive disorder...

In my drawings for Paul's poetry, I wanted to include references to Carroll's books too, and also from my own viewpoint. I tried to include visual nods to Carroll's time as well as to Paul's world. Thank you, Paul, for this challenging and exciting project!

Printed in Great Britain
by Amazon

18460375R00037